Burma Travel Guide

Sightseeing, Hotel, Restaurant & Shopping Highlights

Gary Jennings

Table of Contents

Burma (Myanmar)

Myanmar (also known as Burma) is an emerging tourist destination in Southeast Asia. It lies on the Bay of Bengal and Andaman Sea coast with Bangladesh and India to the west, China to the north, and Laos and Thailand to the east. The country vividly recalls the exotic air of adventure that once romanticised this former British colony. If you wish to explore glittering temples, to listen to tales of myth and legend or to watch holy snakes, now is the time.

The country is rich in natural resources, containing deposits of oil and natural gas, as well as precious stones such as jade. The name "Myanmar" originated during the rule of Kyansittha, one of the most celebrated monarchs of Burmese history.

The culture of Myanmar retains elements of Indian and Chinese influence. Buddhism plays an important role and many of its attractions are sites of devotion. The country has thousands of temples and stupas, many of which date back several millennia to the time of the Buddha. There are an estimated 150,000 practicing monks and nuns in the country. Yet the trappings of a Colonial past linger in architecture and other influences.

Culture

The ethnic Burmese, also known as the Bamar, represents about 30 million or 60 percent of the population of Myanmar. They are believed to have Chinese-Tibetan roots, but have settled in the upper and central plains of the country. India exerts a strong cultural influence over this group and this expresses itself in a number of fields, including architecture, art, the sciences and philosophy. There is a clear relationship between the Pali script used by the Bamar, and Sanskrit.

The next largest groups are the Shan, who live mainly in the valley region and the Kayin or Karen, who live in the delta lands near the border. Smaller ethnic groupings include the Kachin, who live near the border with India and Tibet, the Chin and the Mon who are related to the Khmer people.

The people of Myanmar place strong emphasis on dance and music, as forms of cultural expression. A number of traditional instruments are utilized including, the Khaju thin, a conch shell that is blown, various types of flutes and drums and also the saung or Myanmar harp. Music was strongly associated with the worship of nats or spirits that preceded Buddhism. Other traditional crafts include metalwork and woodcarving. The Kachin people are renowned for the quality of their weaving.

Buddhist traditions date back more than 2000 years in Myanmar and still play an important role in the daily lives of its people. Just under 90 percent of the population subscribe to Buddhism as a way of life. Traditionally monasteries have been responsible for educating the youth and there is strong adherence to Buddhist events such as the Buddhist lent, when secular celebrations such as weddings are forbidden. A modest portion of the population practice Christianity, Islam, Hinduism or other faiths such as the traditional animism.

Despite the country's isolationist stance towards foreigners, the average person is friendly and helpful towards strangers.

Location & Orientation

With a size of 676,577 square km, Myanmar, previously known as Burma is the largest country in Southeast Asia. It is bounded by Bangladesh and India to the west, China and Laos to the northeast and Thailand to the east.

To the west, Myanmar is bounded by the Indian Ocean. Its coastline is 2,800 km long.

The administrative capital of Myanmar is Naypyitaw, an urban area that was created less than fifteen years ago, but various other cities, such as Bagan, Mrauk-U, Amarapura, Mandalay and Yangon had served as capital for part or all of the region. Most recently, under British rule, Yangon or Rangoon as it used to be known had been the capital of Burma. Centrally located, Naypyitaw is divided into various zones, some of which are off limits to foreigners. The local currency is the kyat.

Much of Myanmar's landscape is taken up by rainforest and mountain ranges. Geographically the country divides into three mountain ranges, the RakhineYoma, the BagoYoma and the Shan Plateau. The people of Myanmar have settled mainly in the Irrawady River basin. The river ends in an extensive delta system that covers a territory of 240km by 210km. Myanmar's highest peak, located in Khakaborazi National Park in the north of the country, is Hkakabo Razi, which reaches an impressive 5,881 m.

Climate & When to Visit

Myanmar enjoys a tropical monsoon climate with the rainy season occurring between May and October. This brings strong winds, thunderstorms and a daily pounding of heavy rain, particularly in the coastal regions, where annual rainfall of up to 5000 mm can be experienced.

There is a central dry zone that sees considerably less rainfall, but the ideal months to visit would be the dry cool season, which occurs between December and February. The months of March and April are hottest, but still dry, although the humidity factor does play a role. As Myanmar is mountainous, altitude also affects the climate.

Bagan sees considerably less rain, even during the wet season, as it is sheltered by the proximity of the Rakhine Yoma Mountains to the west. The maximum temperatures exceed 30 degrees Celsius throughout the year, but the nights are cooler from December to February. Mandalay is also located within the central dry zone and receives only 776 mm per year. Here maximum temperatures of up to 38 degrees Celsius have been recorded in April, the warmest month. In the cooler months from December to February, temperatures between 11 degrees Celsius minimum and 27 to 28 degrees maximum can be expected. The climate in Yangon is hottest in April, when temperatures around 30 degrees Celsius are expected, but highs of up to 40 degrees Celsius are not unusual. In January, temperatures between 25 degrees Celsius and 17.9 degrees Celsius can be experienced.

Sightseeing Highlights

Yangon

Yangon is one of the most exotic and cosmopolitan cities Myanmar has to offer. Once the capital of British Burma, the city still boasts some of the best examples of British Colonial architecture and counts among its residents, Indians, Chinese and Anglo-Burmese. Despite it being the largest city in Myanmar, it is surrounded by parks, lakes and tropical vegetation.

Yangon dates back to 1755, when it was founded by King Alaungpaya, but it remained a modest town until the period of British rule around 1885. The British annexed the town, renamed it Rangoon and elevated it to the status of capital. A number of colonial style structures date back to this period, but it is also home to several noteworthy Buddhist temples. Shwedagon Pagoda or Paya, to use the Burmese term is one of the most awe-inspiring of Buddhist temples.

Other religious attractions include Sule Paya and Chaukhtatgyi Paya, where you will be able to view an enormous reclining Buddha. On University Avenue, you will find the Colonial style mansion of Aung San SuuKyi, the Nobel Peace Prize Laureate who was only recently released from the restrictions of her house arrest. Another unusual building is the Musmeah Yeshua Synagogue in Inya Road, dating back to 1896. Yangon currently has a population of 20 Jews, considerably less than the community of 4,000, most of Iraqi or Iranian descent, who had resided in the city at the time of World War Two.

One way of exploring the city is via the Yangon Circular Train, which only costs $1. The route takes approximately 3 hours. About 45 minutes away from Yangon, is the luxury resort of Ngapali beach, which offers golf, fishing, snorkelling and volleyball as well as massage and spa treatments.

Shwedagon Pagoda

Center of the city, Yangon (Rangoon), Myanmar

Legend suggests that Shwedagon Pagoda was constructed 2600 years ago when Buddha met two merchants who were brothers, Taphussa and Bhallika met Lord Gautama Buddha in 588BC. The holy man gave them eight hairs and these were enshrined in the pagoda, which was erected on Singuttara Hill. The hairs were presented to Okkalapa, the King of Burma, whereupon they were found to have various miraculous properties.

The pagoda, which is located in Yangon, is regarded to be one of the most sacred places in all of Myanmar. It has suffered some damage in its long history, most notably during a powerful earthquake in 1768. On various occasions attempts were made to loot the massive bell. Philip de Britoy Nicote of Portugal stole the 30-ton bell, but lost it to the Bago River in the early 1600s. Centuries later, a similar theft by the British suffered a similar fate, but on that occasion the bell was recovered by natives, after they extracted a promise from the British to restore it to the stupa. At night, the Shwendagon Pagoda is lit with sodium vapor lamps.

The building is enormous and elaborately decorated. It is visible from virtually anywhere in Yangon. Four covered walkways provide access to the platform and, while the western, southern and northern walkways offer the easier options of escalators or elevators, the eastern walkway is the most picturesque, as it passes various monasteries and also vendors selling devotional items. The items sold include flowers, Buddhas and incense.

The stupa is fitted with a giant bell, which is covered with gold leaf and re-gilded on an annual basis. The hti or spire decoration is spread across seven tiers. It is covered with gold plate and encrusted with 1100 diamonds. This is topped by the Diamond Orb, which contains another 4351 diamonds.

There are various rituals associated with a visit. As with all temples, visitors have to remove their shoes. It should also be circled clockwise and the starting point is determined by which day of the week the visitor was born. Admission is $5.

Botatoung Pagoda

Corner of Strand Road and Botahtaung Pagoda Road Downtown, Yangon (Rangoon), Myanmar

With its glitteringly detailed artwork, Botahtaung Pagoda is one of the three most visited pagodas in the city of Yangon. The temple has an attractive riverside location, near the local jetty and the surrounding grounds are tranquil and well maintained. There are a number of historical artefacts and a large variety of statues inside the 48 m high temple. You need to pass through a hall covered in gold leaf and a dazzling glass mosaic walkway to reach its relic, a hair of Buddha, enshrined in a glass. A side building contains a Mandalay style Buddha seated on a jewelled throne. The building suffered damage during World War Two, but was repaired in the 1950s. Admission is $3.

Tomb of Bahadur Shah Zafar

8 ZiWaKa Rd., Yangon (Rangoon), Myanmar

Bahadur Shah Zafar inherited a crumbling realm to become the last Mogul Emperor of the Timurid Dynasty, ending four centuries of rule. For his role in the Indian Rebellion of 1857, he was exiled to Rangoon, where he died on 7 November 1862, at the age of 87. A bamboo fence was erected around the grave, but it was left unmarked by the British.

The original gravesite was rediscovered in 1991, when a construction crew digging to lay pipes, discovered the brick-lined tomb. A prayer hall was erected and the grave is now a site of pilgrimage for Burmese Muslims as well as Indians. In 2012, the Indian premier Dr. Manmohan Singh visited the shrine.

Kyaikto (Golden Rock) Pagoda

One of Myanmar's most spectacular and distinctive sites is that of the precariously perched Golden Rock Pagoda. According to legend, a single hair of Buddha holds the rock to its base. The bus trip from Yangon to the town of Kyaikhto lasts four and a half hours and costs around $8.12, after which you will probably take an hour-long truck ride to the pagoda, costing $2.50. The last part of the journey is a rather strenuous walk.

There are various viewing platform, pagodas, Buddha shrines and shrines dedicated to nat spirits.

The rock is covered with gold leaf. It is particularly impressive at sunset. Using a camera at the rock costs an additional $3.

Thanbyuzayat (Death Railway)

History buffs with a particular interest in World War Two may wish to visit Thanbyuzayat, terminal of the infamous Death Railway linking Thailand to Burma. It is alleged to have claimed the lives of over 80,000 workers, which included Burmese laborers as well as prisoners of war. The graves of 3771 Allied servicemen can be viewed in the Thanbyuzayat War Cemetery and the town also has a Death Railway Museum. The museum includes various artifacts from the era and even one of the original locomotives, gifted by the Japanese. Although the War Cemetery is challenging to reach, a number of operators in Yangon do offer tours to the area.

There are two other Allied War Cemeteries in Myanmar. The Htauk Kyant War Memorial Cemetery is located in Mingaladon Township, 32 km from Yangon and commemorates 27,000 fallen Commonwealth soldiers from various conflicts. Yangon War Memorial Cemetery is smaller, with only 1450 graves and can be found on Pyay Road in Sangyoung Township.

Bagan

Located in the north of the country, along the banks of the Irrawaddy River, Bagan was first settled around 200 AD, but rose to prominence in the period between 800 and 1300 AD, when it became the capital of the Pagan Empire. At the height of that era, it may have had as many as 200,000 citizens and well over 10,000 structures of religious significance. These included about 1000 stupas, 10,000 temples and 3,000 monasteries.

The Pagan Empire was the first political entity to unify the people of Myanmar into one single nation. It fell in the years between 1287 and 1297, under the impact of Mongol invasion and the rise of the Myinsaing Kingdom, which compelled the abdication of the Pagan king. Just over 2,200 temples and stupas remain.

There are various ways to experience Bagan. The most expensive is by hot air balloon. For $295, you can get a bird's eye view of the former capital's layout. For between $14 and $18, you can enjoy a tour via horse-drawn cart. The cheapest ways of exploring the region is by renting a bicycle for just $1.50 per day or by taking the local pick-up for just over $1.

Ananda Temple

Bagan, Myanmar

Ananda Temple was built in 1091 by Kyansittha, a famous king in Burma's history.

A legend suggests that the builders, eight monks, were killed upon completion to prevent them from duplicating the structure. The name of the temple means 'endless wisdom' in Sanskrit and it is one of the most highly regarded buildings of its kind in Myanmar. The symmetry of its layout is truly impressive. The architecture features a blend of Indian and Mon styles.

There are four standing Buddha images, facing respectively south, north, east and west and various niches feature Buddhas of more modest proportions. The larger Buddhas subtly change expression as you approach them. The four main Buddha's are adorned with gold leaf and each bears a different name, associated with a specific state of nirvana. There are also frescoes that depict the full life cycle of Buddha from birth to death. Like all pagodas in Myanmar, it features an ornament known as ahti at the pinnacle. The distribution of windows built into the walls provides natural ventilation.

Although damaged by an earthquake in 1975, the temple has been restored and is regularly maintained. In 1990, its 900th anniversary was celebrated. There is a field museum near Ananda Temple.

Mount Popa

About 50km southeast of Bagan, the enigmatic volcano known as Mount Popa can be found. It is extinct, its last volcanic activity estimated at 250,000 years ago.

Reaching a height of 1518 m above sea level, Mount Popa is strongly associated with the Nat spirits that dominated belief systems in Myanmar before the advent of Buddhism and endure to some extent alongside of it. According to legend, Nats are the spirits of prominent or heroic beings that continue to serve the interests of mankind after their physical demise. The beliefs were merged with Buddhist principles. A symbolic act of this had been the instalment of 37 Nat images near the sacred pagoda of Shwezigon, by King Anawrahta. The gesture could be seen as a truce after years spent trying to suppress belief in the Nats.

Mount Popa is composed of basalt and it has fertile soil and numerous streams of water. The name means 'mountain of flowers' in Sanskrit and it is now a National Park.
Its most distinctive feature is Taung Kalat, a volcanic plug that is now the location of a Buddhist monastery. It offers a breathtaking view of the surrounding landscape, but to reach the summit, visitors have to ascend up 777 steps. Taung Kalat is also home to a community of wild Macaque monkeys.

Mandalay

Mandalay is the second largest city of Myanmar and had been the last capital of an independent Burma. It was established in 1857 along the eastern bank of the Irrawady River, by Mandalay hill.

Even under British rule, it remained significant as a center for the Burmese cultural identity, maintaining old traditions of theatre and artistic expression. During World War Two, it was occupied by the Japanese and suffered considerably damage. The royal palace citadel, for example, was completely destroyed.

The city is home to several monasteries as well as a number of pagodas. Shwenandaw Monastery is noteworthy as it features a number of teak woodcarvings that depict various scenes from Buddhist myth. It was built during the 19th century by King Mindon Min and his successor, King Thibaw Min. Minguin temple is an enigma. It is incomplete and unsafe, due to the ravages of recent earthquakes, but contains the world's largest and heaviest hung bell, which weighs in at around 90 tonnes. The bell was cast in 1790, at the commission of King Bodawpaya, but with his untimely death, the temple was never finished.

Snake Pagoda (HmwePaya)

Paleik, Mandalay, Myanmar

There is an intriguing legend associated with this pagoda. The monk tending the devotional area noticed two pythons curling around a statue of Buddha and sought to remove them.

The snakes kept returning, until the monk realized that they had to be the reincarnated souls of past monks. The resident pythons now enjoy elevated status, with all their needs cared for. A daily ritual is the 11am cleansing in a bath of flower petals. The original snakes associated with the pagoda have since died, but their remains were preserved.

Kuthodaw Pagoda

Kuthodaw Pagoda is located at the foot of Mandalay Hill. Its most striking feature is the largest book in the world, which takes the shape of 729 marble slabs, each representing a page of the Tipitaka. This contains three groups of text widely regarded as the Pali Canon of Theravada Buddhism. It was built between 1860 and 1868 and includes a covered approach, with accompanying frescoes, ornately carved doors of teak as well as a garden filled with fragrant starflower trees.

Between 1885 and 1890, the site was occupied by British troops and many of its treasures such as bells and jewels were looted. Through various initiatives in subsequent years, some of its splendor had been restored for posterity.

U Bein's Bridge

One of the main attractions of Amarapura is U Bein's Bridge. Spanning 1.2km across the Taungthaman Lake, it is the longest wooden bridge in the world, featuring over a thousand posts of teak.

Constructed of teak wood, it is well over 100 years old. These days, it includes a number of souvenir and craft vendors. Amarapura is about 10km south of Mandalay.

Mandalay Marionettes Theatre

66th St., Between 26th & 27th St., Mandalay, Myanmar
Tel: 95-2-34446

Marionettes are an integral part of social culture in Myanmar and in olden times they played many roles. Puppet theatre was used to enact news of the capital to rural communities, but they would also be employed when bad news had to be passed on to the monarch or to deliver a reprimand without directly insulting the recipient. The marionettes were elaborately costumed, carefully jointed and decorated and often fitted with real human hair. There are 28 specific characters, which include the King, the Queen, a Magician, a Hermit, a Palace Ogre, three Jokers as well as various courtiers, servants, spiritual or mythical beings and even animals.

To experience this traditional art form, as delivered by a group of skilled and dedicated practitioners, do book a performance at the Mandalay Marionettes Theatre. A show lasts approximately one hour and includes music and dance, based around the telling of traditional folk tales. One performance costs around $12 per person. The venue also sells authentic marionettes to the public.

Grottes de Po Win Daung

Village Minzu, Monywa, Myanmar

Located about 135 km northwest of Mandalay and 40km from Monywa, this network of caves showcases a variety of statues of Buddha, as well as paintings and frescoes. The facade is of a giant elephant and there are a number of impressive Buddhas inside, some carved into the rock, while others had been sculpted at another location and transported to the caves. The frescoes are fairly well maintained, considering the fact that they are between 600 and 700 years old. There is also a community of monkeys at the site. Admission is $5.

Pyin OoLwin

Located about 67 km east of Mandalay at an altitude of about 1000 m, Pyin OoLwin began as a military outpost during the period of British rule and it retains a decidedly anglicised character. It features a number of Colonial buildings, such as the governor's Summer Palace and the Purcell Clock Tower, which dates back to 1936. Another quaint feature is the mode of transportation - attractive horse-drawn stagecoaches that are unique to Pyin OoLwin.

The surrounding land is utilized for the cultivation of coffee beans, extensive mulberry orchards to support the cultivation of silk as well as a flower industry that focussed heavily on the chrysanthemum, the aster and the gladiolus.

Other local products are vegetables, strawberries, pineapples and wine. A research center in the area studies various indigenous herbs that have medicinal properties. One of the nearby attractions is Dadtaw Kyaint waterfall, an impressive sight at over 30m high. It empties into a beautifully rejuvenating pool. Also near Pyin OoLwin, is Penkchin Mhyan cave, where thousands of Buddha images can be seen. It is a site of pilgrimage for Buddhists.

National Kandawgyi Botanical Gardens

Pyin U Lwin, PyinOoLwin (Maymyo), Myanmar

An important attraction is the National Kandawgyi Botanical Gardens. It was established in 1915 by Alex Roger with the considerable help of Lady Charlotte Wheeler Cuffe, the wife of an Imperial officer stationed in the area, who had a considerable knowledge of botany. Drawing on the advice of influential acquaintances such as Sir Frederick Moore, director of the Irish National Botanical garden as well as her own experiences as a botanical watercolorist, she designed the layout of the garden, which was based on Kew Gardens.

The collection at the National Kandawgyi Botanical Gardens includes well over 500 species of indigenous trees, 75 species of bamboo and over 300 indigenous orchid species.

Also represented are roses, water lilies and crotons. Besides plants, the gardens also offer a home to several endangered animal species such as Eld's Deer, the Takin, the Burmese Star Tortoise and the Hog Deer. There is an aviary, which includes peacock and a variety of other birds. The facility has a Fossil Museum, a Petrified Wood Museum and a Butterfly Museum, which features species from Nepal, Japan and even South America. The Gardens include a picturesque pagoda, an observation tower and a tearoom. Originally only 30 acres, the gardens have been extended on various occasions to its current dimensions of 437 acres. The surroundings are peaceful and meticulously maintained. Admission is $5 for tourists.

Mrauk U

From around 1431, Mrauk U was the capital of a kingdom that included a substantial portion of Bangladesh, the state of Rakhine and the lower half of western Burma. The name of the city, which means Monkey's Egg, allegedly refers to a legend of a monkey that had gifted an egg to Buddha. The city's expansion led to the construction of many temples and pagoda's of which the Shittaung Pagoda serves as prime example. The temple was built in 1535 by King Minbar, one of the most celebrated monarchs of the Arakanese kingdom, as it was known and contains numerous small images, as well as various shrines dedicated to kings and queens from different periods of the city's history. Various mythical beings and human activities are also depicted. Shittaung Pagoda remains well preserved.

Within the Royal Palace, you will find the Archaeological Museum, which showcases artifacts such as coins, paintings and Buddhas. The city saw the reign of 48 kings over a period of 355 years. The site is surrounded by hills and mountains characterized by navigable passes. The Aungdat Chaung River provided access to the western coast. The environment includes various coastal, wilderness and wetland habitats. A rare flower, the Thazin, is found in this region. A government permit, costing $5, is needed to visit Mrauk U.

Putao

http://www.putaotrekkinghouse.com/

Putao, the northernmost town of Myanmar is for much of the year, only accessible by air. Located in the Kachin State, it features spectacular mountain views. This includes Mount Hkakaborazi, which is at 5881m the highest peak in Southeast Asia. The Hkakaborazi National Park was established in 1996 and is home to various types of endangered indigenous butterflies, a number of orchid species, as well as the Takin, a rare mammal that is a regarded as somewhere between a goat and ox.

Also native to the region are the Tarongs, a nearly vanished race of pygmies measuring between 140 and 149cm. Isolated and reduced to an estimated 69 individuals, the community still survive through a hunter-gatherer lifestyle and enjoy limited contact with the outside world.

The district of Putao has a British outpost, Fort Hertz, but this has not been manned since the 1940s.

Mt. Phunggan is a popular venue for trekking and mountaineering, while the turbulent waters of the Maykha and Malika Rivers draws river rafting enthusiasts. Putao is connected to Machambaw via the 211m Malikha Suspension Bridge. Machanbaw features a rock formation known as the stone dragon. Local crafts can be bought at Myoma Market.

Inle Lake

Located in the Shan state, 330 km to the southeast of Mandalay, Inle Lake is worth a visit for a number of reasons. Although it is the second largest lake in Myanmar, Inle is shallow and supports dense growth of reed beds and other floating plant like. For this reason, the fishermen who ply their trade here have developed a unique and highly memorable style of leg rowing.

The lake has a hot spring along the north-western shore and is home to nine fish species such as the cross-banded dwarf danio and the Lake Inledanio that are found nowhere else. Between November and January, large numbers of migratory seagulls pass through the region as well.

The lake has a human population of around 70,000, scattered across numerous small villages and representing an interesting mix of ethnic diversity which includes Shan, Bamar, Danu, Kaya, Taungthu and Taungyou people.

Most of the inhabitants live in simple bamboo dwellings on stilts. A daily market, known as the five-day-market, sells local produce and crafts. The venue rotates between five different locations, one of which is the lake itself, when the boats are transformed to mini-stalls. Inphaw Kone, which is west of Nampan Village, is well known for the high quality of its weaving.

Recommendations for the Budget Traveller

Places to Stay

Eastern Hotel

194/196 Bo MyatTun Street, Pazundaung Township,
Yangon (Rangoon), Myanmar
Tel: 95 1 293815
http://www.myanmareasternhotel.com/

The Eastern Hotel is within easy walking distance from
the Bogyoke Aung San Market, Sule Pagoda, Botahtaung
Pagoda, Central Railway Station and a variety of
shopping opportunities.

Rooms include a mini-bar, fridge, hairdryer, bathroom facilities, satellite TV and air-conditioning. There is a restaurant and the hotel offers free high-speed Internet. Accommodation begins at $45 per night and includes breakfast.

Central Hotel Yangon

335/357, Bogyoke Aung San Road | Pabedan Township, Yangon (Rangoon), Myanmar
Tel: 95-1-241001
http://www.centralhotelyangon.com/

Central Hotel Yangon is conveniently located near several attractions such as the Sule Pagoda and Bogyoke market. While the decor recalls vintage styles, rooms are large and comfortable. Staff members are described as friendly and accommodating. Rooms include air-conditioning, bathtub and shower facilities, a mini-bar and satellite TV with an additional movie option. Accommodation begins at $80 and includes a buffet style breakfast.

Kumudara Hotel

Corner Of 5th Street &Dawna Street, Pyu Saw Htee Qtr.,
Bagan, Myanmar
Tel: 061 65142
http://www.kumudara-bagan.com/

Located near several of the distinctive temples of Bagan,
this small hotel offers a tranquil setting that includes a
swimming pool and attractively landscaped gardens.

Rooms include air-conditioning, a minibar and bathtub
and shower facilities. The hotel also offers spa, massage
and free Internet. The hotel has a restaurant and bar. A
variety of tour options can be organized through
reception. Accommodation begins at $39 a night.

Royal City Hotel

27th Street between 76th and 77th, Mandalay, Myanmar
Tel: +95 0 2 66559

The Royal City Hotel is located near the Mandalay
Marionette Theatre and offers great views of the city,
especially from the rooftop lounge. Rooms include a
fridge, mini-bar, air-conditioning and satellite TV.
Furnishings are basic, but functional and staff members
are described as friendly and helpful. The hotel also has a
back-up generator for power blackouts. Wifi is available
only in the lobby. Accommodation begins at $20 a night
and includes breakfast.

Yoma Cherry Lodge

Lintha Village, Ngapali Beach, Ngapali, Myanmar
Tel: +95 0 43 42339
http://yomacherrylodge.com/

With the idyllic tropical setting of wide beach sand and plenty of tropical palm trees, hotels in the Ngapali Beach area tend to be on the pricey side, but Yoma Cherry Lodge presents a more affordable alternative. The furnishings are light, airy and attractive.

The beach is used by the local fishing community which gives you the opportunity to experience a little of the local culture. Activities include fishing, snorkelling, golf and bicycles for hire. The hotel has a restaurant, a lounge bar and offers free Internet. Accommodation begins at $60 a night and includes breakfast as well as airport transfers.

Places to Eat

Aung Thukha

17 (A) 1st Street, West Shwegondaing, Yangon (Rangoon),
Myanmar
Tel: 01 525194

For a no-frills introduction to Burmese style cuisine, pay a
visit to Aung Thukha. The house specialities are a wide
selection of curries, including duck, pork, fish, beef, goat,
prawn and chicken and these are presented buffet style.
Meals include rice, soup and vegetables. Since portions
are small but cheap, the diner offers a great opportunity
to experiment. Although staff members are not exactly
fluent in English, the upside is that you will have the
opportunity to soak up some real local flavor. Expect to
pay less than $5 for the whole dining experience of two
people.

Monsoon Restaurant

85-87,Theinbyu Road, Botataung Tsp, Yangon (Rangoon),
Myanmar
Tel: +95 1 295224,
http://www.monsoonmyanmar.com/

Monsoon features a medley of dishes from Laos,
Thailand, Vietnam, Cambodia and Myanmar. Some of the
menu items include Burmese tempura, fish cakes, chicken
curry, grilled king prawns, stir-fried squid with
vegetables, stir-fried beef with bamboo and sesame seeds,
stir-fried pork with lime and coconut sauce, grilled
eggplant salad with shrimp, chicken wings in caramel
sauce, fried shrimp cakes, sweet and sour spare ribs, a
selection of soups and a monsoon mixed grill which
includes pork, beef, chicken, sausage and potatoes.
Portions are generous. Expect to pay around $12 for one
person's full meal, plus drinks. Upstairs is a gift shop that
sells crafts from a women's co-operative. Monsoon is
affiliated to Green Restaurant in Mandalay.

Boost Bar @Inya Day Spa

16/2 Inya Road, Yangon (Rangoon) Kamayut Township,
Myanmar
Tel: 01 503375

Boost Bar specializes in healthy revitalizing smoothies.
Most are based around berries such as strawberries,
blueberries and raspberries, and honey is used as
sweetener in place of sugar. Do also enjoy some of the spa
treatments such as foot massages. Expect to pay between
$3.50 and $4.

The Moon Vegetarian Restaurant

North of Ananda Temple, Bagan, Myanmar
Tel: 061-60481

The Moon Vegetarian restaurant offers both inside and
outside seating in a relaxing environment. The cuisine
makes creative use of all manner of ingredients while
staying within the concept of vegetarian cuisine. Some of
the menu items include pumpkin soup, coconut vegetable
soup, green papaya salad, pumpkin curry, winter melon
curry, tomato curry, fried cashew nuts with vegetables
and sweet and sour vegetables with bamboo shoot or
potatoes, as well as a selection of fruit smoothies. With
most items priced at between $1.75 and $2.50, you can
expect to enjoy a meal that is both tasty and affordable.
Meals are usually rounded off with Tamarind candies, a
treat that is unique to Bagan. No alcohol is served.

Marie Min

27th Street, between 74th and 75th Street, Mandalay, Myanmar

Marie Min serves vegetarian cuisine, prepared in a blend of Indian and Burmese styles. Menu items include pumpkin curry, mixed vegetable curry and Indian staples such as dahl, chapatti and raita. For beverages, try the lassies, made with homemade yoghurt or the juices. Expect to pay between $3 and $6 for a dinner. Opposite Marie Min is Rain Forest, an affordable Thai-style diner run by the same extended family.

Places to Shop

Bogyoke Aung San Market, Yangon

Bogyoke Aung San Market can be found in a colonial style building in the Pabedan township of Yangon. Originally known as Scott's Market, after a British civil servant James George Scott, it was built in 1926, occupies two floors and features almost 2000 stalls. Since it presents a wide variety of souvenirs, crafts, antiques and art, the market has become a major attraction for foreign tourists. Jewellery traders can be found near the center of the market, and they can offer great deals on rubies, jade and other precious stones.

From the antique dealers, coins, postage stamps and old banknotes can be purchased. Other items include paintings, wooden items, fans, maps, handbags, bags, T-shirts, hats and also longhis, traditional sarong-like garments that the people of Myanmar favour. A new wing features items such as food, medicine and clothing.

Lacquerwork in Bagan

Bagan is well known for the quality of its lacquer work products. It was highly prized by the British during their rule of Burma. If done expertly, the lacquer waterproofs an item, protects it against the ravages of heat and beautifies its finish. Besides various small market stalls and tourist shops, there are a number of recommended stops for lacquer work.

The Chan Thar Lacquer ware Workshop offers a wide range of products items ranging from functional kitchenware to furniture and ornamental pieces such as jewellery products. They can be found along main road in the MyinKa Par part of Bagan. In the same area, Golden Cuckoo Lacquer ware Workshop features the work of four generations of skilled craftsmen and sells items such as cups, bowls and tray. You may even see one of the artisans at work, as they do not mind an audience. Moe Moe Family Lacquer ware along Main Road in the Ywar Thit Quarter combines traditional and modern influences in their style.

The Golden Bagan Lacquer ware Shop can tackle large pieces such as treasure chests as well as smaller novelty items. They are located in Khaye Main Road in New Bagan. Other workshops to visit include Ever Stand Lacquer ware Workshop in Wetkyi-in Village, Tun Handcrafted Lacquer ware in Khan Laung Quarter, U Ba Nyein Lacquer ware Workshop in Myo Thit and Shwe La Yaung Lacquer ware Shop in the South Quarter.

Shwe War Thein Handicrafts Shop, Bagan

East of Tharabar Gate, Taung Be Village, Old Bagan

If you wish to explore Burma of old through trinkets of the past, do pay a visit to the Shwe War Thein Handicrafts Shop. The items featured include a large variety of antiques and keepsakes such as jewellery, gems, beads, woodcarving, stone carving, chess sets, bronze items and even puppets. Salesmen are highly knowledgeable about the provenance of each item. It is likely to prove a highly entertaining and educational experience.

Buying Artwork in Myanmar

After feasting your eyes on the elaborate devotional art of Myanmar's temples, you may wish to take a modest piece of Burmese art home with you. There are a number of places to look. Near the temples of Bagan, you will usually find a sand painter at work promoting his wares. These may be based on devotional art. Do shop around for the best bargain.

Yangon has several galleries, which sell traditional and modern art and the Strand River Gallery should be one of your first stops. It is located in the Strand Hotel complex at 92 Strand Street and showcases the art of various Burmese artists. Inya Gallery exhibits the work of the award-winning Burmese artist, Aung Myint. New Zero Art Space encourages the fusion of Burmese and foreign styles. It is a non-profit initiative by the artist and teacher Aye Ko. Beik Thano Gallery can be found at 113/3B Kaba Aye Pagoda Road in Bahan, Yangon. Augustine's Antiques in Attiyar St, Yangon, sells a variety of intriguing works including silverware, lacquer ware, brass, copper and bronze items as well as porcelain.

There are a number of local artists from the area selling their paintings and drawings at U Bein's bridge for very reasonable prices. There are also art stalls on the stairway at Mandalay Hill that may be worth a visit.

Shopping in Mandalay

Myanmar is well known for the quality of its gems, particularly jade and Mandalay is a good place to browse through the wares of gem dealers. The Mahar Aung Myay Gems Dealers' Market between 39th Street & 40th Street in the Mahar Aung Myay Township provides an outlet for various wholesalers in gems and jewellery and it is usually possible to get a good bargain here. Gem Palace at 376, corner of 33rd Street and 83rd Street in Chan Aye Thar San Township is a premier location in gems, which offers a wide variety of goods.

For souvenirs, visit Amara Waddy on 493/25, 81st Street, between 35th Street & 36th Street. They sell a number of popular items such as Buddhas and woodcraft. The Man Thiri Market and Zegyo market are located within close proximity of each other near 86th Street, Aung Myay Thar San Township. Zegyo Market is a particular good location to soak up some local flavor in the form of spices, crafts and traditional costumes.

Printed in Great Britain
by Amazon.co.uk, Ltd.,
Marston Gate.